In the Black Inkwell

Samantha Kriese

BookLeaf Publishing

Presentation by *BookLeaf Publishing*

Web: www.bookleafpub.com

E-mail: info@bookleafpub.com

ISBN: 9789357213394

First edition 2023

Will Fade

Will you remember me on day?
When your hair is white
and your age is old?
Will you envision this time,
we call ours now
as you walk on feeble legs
and grasp with wrinkled hands?
Will you still know love then?
Will you recall my name?
Or shall I just be a dream
that will fade one day?

Numbness

I am light
and I am dark.
In my rigid chaos
I am marked.
In my flesh
my body sustains.
But to break the skin
and let the matter
flow
away…

The beauty of the life
to let it all go.
The numbness you feel
as you contemplate;
then yourself you will hate
as those thoughts
you feel in your core,
you feel you cannot escape.

I'm Afraid

I'm afraid for what lies beyond future's bend.
I'm afraid that they are trying to kill our
imaginations.
I'm afraid of the cookie-cutter they will push us
down with.
I'm afraid of the ignorance that plagues so many
of you.
I'm afraid of the eyes that glaze toward wrong
doing.
I'm afraid for all children now and those to
come.
I'm afraid for all kind hearts that get mauled,
until they choose to end it all.

I'm afraid of the sickness that needs a cure.
I'm afraid of the entitlement that rots your soul.
I'm afraid of the hate that flows so freely
through your veins.
I'm afraid of the greed that sours your brain.
I'm afraid of the lies we live among,
whose truths we will never see the other side of.

Words You Said

My muscles tighten
as my hands shake
with the itch to impact.
My mind sweats thoughts
that I would normally regret.
My throat restricts
to keep my roar at bay.
My eyes glaze
with desire for destruction.
The sour,
salty taste,
jaw clenched.
The sound of blood
rushing to my head.

It was the words you said.

In the Black Inkwell

In the black ink well
awaits the elixir that pairs
with the medium.
The obsidian liquid
stains the starch page,
creating the power of the word.

The words come alive
with some thought
and a black ink well.
The life blood to the pen,
a writer's champion.

Remembering the Fair

You walk on the grass that itches your ankles,
the scent of corndogs and funnel cakes
already clinging to your hair and clothes.
Sounds of music,
screaming,
mechanical shifting
as gigantic thrillers trap entertained fair-goers
in their bellies.
The food tastes better than its tantalizing smell,
loved by all,
even the bees.
Summer is the county fair's home,
but it never stays long,
always leaving you wanting more.

Gravity of Meaning

Hostile in nature,
that's important to remember,
experience makes the heart grow harder,
youth is a fruit that takes time to ripen,
gloom is a romantic way to say poor weather
or mood,
a cluster of gossiping people are lesser
than a cluster of cows standing in dung,
intentions are better left quiet until carried
through,
personality should be personal,
not copied,
drowning in philosophies,
stating harsh words won't improve your posture.

Grit

Winds of time blow away
some of the grit,
but some grit sticks
like gravel lodged in your knee,
latched so deep
it marries the bone.

And it poisons the blood,
contaminating the flow,
eventually spoiling the brain.
Toxins pooling into the heart
and the everlasting soul.

The grit never smooths,
you just meld to it,
until the grit becomes you,
the death of forgiveness.

Impact

We were made with such potential.
Promises as grand as the sun.
Our bodies were to remain pure,
but tainted and shadowed we did become;
and in the ways of the flesh,
we did succumb.
We were given the world,
but we still made bombs.
Generations keep coming,
small bodies growing,
learning.
Impacts of self-made destructions
left in the galaxy of a child's eye.
We were made for better purposes,
but we unashamedly slump on the
disappointment line.
When shall we ever be satisfied?

This Body is Earthly

I dreamt of poetry,
and words only whispered in dreams
came to life around me
and within me.
Calling out to the universe
that I
was just a simple thing.
Proclaiming,
all the same,
that I loved all life
as a mother loves
and cares for a child.
But I am no mother,
only a child.
We come unto this existence
crowning
like the sun in dawn's light.
I then cried out,
pleading,
"Awaken my heart
to a greater understanding,
though this body is earthly,
the soul within,
it is mighty."

Wordless

His love
is a poetry
I could never write.

Life Reads like a Poem

Life happens in epics,
and it happens in stanzas.
It happens in chapters,
and it happens in caesuras.
It's in the rhythm and flow
and the skin of your soul.

Our journeys are made of hyperboles
and litotes.
Feel your internal rhythm,
for it beats differently in all of us.
Take on the paradox.
Make peace with the refrain.

Life happens in epics,
and it happens in stanzas.
It happens in chapters,
and it happens in caesuras.
It's in the rhythm and flow
and the skin of your soul.

Ancient Attributions

The past doesn't die.
It thrives.
We live among its skeletons,
don't we?
Existing among history's caverns
and ancient attributions.
Present life flourishing
in the sunken anatomy
of a bygone colossus.
Though it surrounds us,
silently telling its stories,
we show little regard
for the former.
All the while,
time devours us
until at last
our bones contribute
to the antiquity.

The Nature of Waves

You came in like a wave
collapsing upon the shore.
A wave,
nothing more.
You beckoned,
exasperatingly begged!

But I know the nature of waves
and your brief
redundant desires.
You long for a taste of the shore,
nothing more.

Your Darkness

Your heart is a realm of shadows.
So many barriers to get passed
just to reach the core.
You share only half of the truth.
What lurks in your darkness?

Should Have Learned

There was a rasp to the wind,
an unwelcome exertion of force.
A storm was upon us,
in the hour of which the night knew so well.
The lightening that blinded,
thunder that crawled up the spine.
The rain that would drowned all.
The end was coming for us.
We told the sky to leave us be
as the clouds and first droplets did mock us.
The world was about to pay for its sins,
but even then, people did not learn
for they continued to sin.
Even when the curses rattled Egypt,
when the plagues reduced Europe to rubbish,
when the wars left nothing but rifts...
we did not learn.
Now that it is too late,
we see with full consciousness
what is coming for us.
We should have learned!
We should have learned!

On Tuesday

What did I do on Tuesday?
Well
I waited for you.
Your Monday promises meant nothing
on Tuesday.
Why should they?
It was another day after all.
Whole worlds can be created
and destroyed in a day.
That
is what happened on Tuesday.

Tuesday,
was the loose spigot on the cask
of Monday's hopes.
The day of splintered destinies.
And you,
you spoke not a word on Tuesday.
So
I decided not to play your games anymore.
Hello Wednesday.

A Fisherman's Joy

The Angler baited and cast,
as his vessel did drift.
Extracting finned creature
after scaly beast
from the watery world.
A grip on the gills,
haul on the hook,
he jerked the line.
Another nibble,
patience,
quiet,
ready,
STRIKE!
Reeling in he knew
as the wire went taught
after a wiggle
that he would feast
on an edible, aquatic dinner
giving the bait another jiggle.

The Melancholy Prince

He reclines upon the written works,
this prince of poets.
The papers are torn, crinkled
and of thinning resolve.
They are discolored with age, pain
and his victims,
the hemorrhaging ink bottles.
His hands were of the same nature.
Face streaked in grief
and inky lamentations.
Here be the melancholy prince,
burdened with thoughts
and the written word.
He sees beauty in the dark,
with hooded eyes
and a sullen heart.
A manner so morose,
there wouldn't be much more excitement
in a storm.
Drowning in his own sludgy emotions
he lives,
closed off from the great wide world.

Hair slick and speckled
from ink coated hands gripping it viscously.
He wears his sorrows like a crown.
He takes solace in nothing,
except his gothic pleasures.

Season of Change

Under the sepia sun
stands the drama of Autumn.
Fading life in a blaze of color,
auburn stems weaken
and leaves learn to be free.
Crisp winds prophesize change,
abundant clusters of amber crunch
underfoot.
In the breezy autumnal brilliance,
comes a brisk rustling.
The trees converse
in harsh whispers,
speaking in languages of orange, red
and gold.

Night's Decorum

The night is her house,
carefully placing her garland of stars.
The sun is disinterested in her art,
but the moon loves it so.
Until the pearl of night grows dull,
she will bedizen the sky.

www.ingramcontent.com/pod-product-compliance
Lightning Source LLC
Chambersburg PA
CBHW051721130826
49812CB00034B/1292
9789357213394